This book is dedicated to my second born son, Tyler Zachary, my angel in heaven.

A Close Up Look at

Zion National Park

By Josie Zayac

Zion National Park, whose name
means "promised land",
is a desert full of canyons,
mesas, rivers, cliffs, and sand.

Take a close look.

What do you see?

It's called lichen- made of fungi and algae. Lichen grows on rocks or trees.

Take a close look.
What do you see?

Regular grass- it is not!

It's scouring rush- used to clean pots.

Take a close look.
What do you know?

Maidenhair fern needs little soil to grow.

Take a close look.
What do you see?

The sacred datura,
Oh, so pretty.

Take a close look.
What do you see?

A weeping rock.
Don't cry for me!

Rain and snow
from way up high
soak through the sandstone
and make it cry.

Take a close look.
What do you see?

Checkerboard mesa- where mountain goats might be.

Take a close look.
What do you see?

The spines of a cactus, so prickly.

Take a close look.
What do you see?

Ancient petroglyphs.
How old can they be?

Perhaps 7,000 years old.
Older than you and me!

Take a close look.
What do you see?

A couple of
lizards.
There are 16
species.

Take a close look.
What good luck!

It's a
deer
mommy,
called a
doe.

And a
daddy,
called
a buck.

Take a close look.
What do you see?
There's so much to do,
so much history.

Go for a hike, enjoy the sight.
Observe the animals.
Be careful- they bite!

Facts about Zion National Park, Utah

- Mormons settled in the area in the 1860s and gave the park its name
- Zion means "promised land"
- Elevations range from 3,666 to 8,726 feet
- Zion officially became a National Park on November 19, 1919
- Zion is located in Utah, along the edge of the Colorado Plateau

Look for other National Park books by Dr. Josie Zayac

- A Close Up Look at Bryce Canyon National Park
- A Close Up Look at Crater Lake National Park
- A Close Up Look at Cuyahoga Valley National Park
- A Close Up Look at Joshua Tree National Park
- A Close Up Look at Redwood National and State Parks
- A Close Up Look at Rocky Mountain National Park
- A Close Up Look at Sequoia National Park
- A Close Up Look at Theodore Roosevelt National Park
- A Close Up Look at Zion National Park

www.ingramcontent.com/pod-product-compliance
Lightning Source LLC
Chambersburg PA
CBHW050930290526
45792CB00002B/956